The New York Reader

By Ann E. Burg

Illustrated by K. L. Darnell

The author would like to thank the members of the Annie Moore Memorial Project
for helping her separate the layers of myth surrounding our nation's first immigrant.

The source for the text of the correspondence between Abraham Lincoln and Grace Bedell came
from the Abraham Lincoln Research Site at http://members.aol.com/RVSNorton1/Lincoln50.html.

Sleeping Bear Press™

310 North Main Street, Suite 300
Chelsea, MI 48118
www.sleepingbearpress.com

© 2008 Sleeping Bear Press is an imprint of Gale, a part of Cengage Learning.

Printed and bound in China.

10 9 8 7 6 5 4 3 2 1

Library of Congress Cataloging-in-Publication Data

Burg, Ann E.
The New York reader / written by Ann Burg ; illustrated by K.L. Darnell. — 1st ed.
p. cm. — (State reader series)
Summary: "Modeled after traditional primers, this book includes individual stories,
riddles, and original poems about New York State. Subjects include Freedom of the
Press; the Harlem Renaissance; and cultural diversity"—Provided by publisher.
ISBN 978-1-58536-349-0
1. New York (State)—Juvenile literature. 2. New York
(State)—Literary collections. 3. Readers (Primary) I. Darnell,
Kathryn. II. Title.
PS3602.U7415N48 2008
810.8'09747—dc22   2008012481

Preface

Hello! Welcome to *The New York Reader*! I was born in Brooklyn and have lived most of my life in New York so I am excited about sharing with you these stories and poems about my home state.

Most of the people you will read about lived a long time ago, but they were once children just like you. History is not a list of names and dates engraved in stone. History is the story of people who lived just as we are living today, people who were once children just as you are, children with hopes and dreams for the future.

The stories, poems, riddles, and pictures that appear in *The New York Reader* are fashioned after early primers which were once used to teach reading. I hope you will enjoy them and share them with your family and friends. Perhaps you will be inspired to write some stories and poems of your own. I hope each of you will grow up to love New York as much as I do!

Your friend,
Ann E. Burg

For my mother,
my first teacher,
and for the children
in the classrooms I visit;
you teach me, too!

ANN

❀

To the memory of Judith Anderson,
extraordinary woman, fine artist, good friend.

KATE

Table of Contents

New York Pledge

I pledge my heart to New York State,
its countryside and cityscapes,
its rolling hills and sparkling sea,
its fields, its farms, and factories.
By concrete path or crystal stream
New Yorkers live and work and dream,
and my heart will always be
glad New York is home to me.

New York Numbers

10 ladybugs were lying on a leaf.
 It suddenly started to rain.
4 ladybugs flew home for umbrellas.
 How many ladybugs remained?

 1 apple in my lunchbox.
 6 in Grandma's pie.
 10 apples in my basket.
How many in my rhyme?

If **3** shy scallops
 invited **2** friends to dine,
how many plates of algae
 would they need at suppertime?

If **6** speckled trout were swimming
in a stream,
and one followed a wiggling worm,
how many would there be?

If **8** busy beavers
were chomping at a tree,
and **4** of them went home to bed,
how many would there be?

If **2** white-bellied bluebirds
perched on a tree
were joined by another **2**,
how many would there be?

Manhattan Riddles

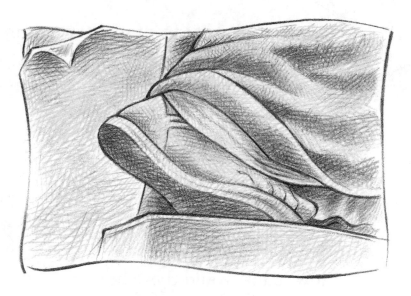

I stand in the waters between
New York and New Jersey.
I was a gift from France to the United
States but I lift my torch for all people.
I wear a crown on my head and
sandals on my feet.
Who am I?

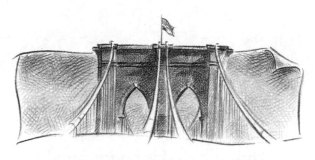

I stretch all the way from
Brooklyn to Manhattan.
Thousands of people cross my
ribbons of steel every day.
Who am I?

I climb 1,250 feet into the sky.
At night colored lights in my towers
celebrate the seasons.
I am one of the most famous buildings
in New York City.
Who am I?

I rumble through dark underground tunnels
bringing people from one end of the
city to the other.
I travel quickly, screeching loudly
and swaying from side to side.
Hold on tight—I give a bumpy ride!
Who am I?

I offer a royal view of the paths, ponds,
and gardens that surround me.
I am also a weather station and an
observatory for young naturalists.
Who am I?

All day long busy people scurry up
and down my marble stairs.
They wait for loved ones beside my
famous four-sided brass clock
or marvel at the stars in my
great domed ceiling.
Who am I?

Hidden State Symbols

State tree: Sugar Maple / State flower: Rose
State bird: Bluebird / State animal: Beaver
State reptile: Snapping turtle
State bush: Lilac

9

The Two Row Wampum Belt

The Two Row Wampum Belt is a symbol of the treaty that the Haudenosaunee entered with seventeenth-century Dutch traders. The Haudenosaunee, also known as the Six Nations, are the native people of what is now known as North America.

For hundreds of years before the Europeans came, the Haudenosaunee lived in harmony with the earth. They depended on the earth for food and shelter and in turn took good care of the earth. When the

Dutch traders came, the Haudenosaunee hoped to share their resources and live in peace.

The Two Row Wampum Belt is made up of two parallel rows of purple wampum and three rows of white wampum. One purple row represents the Haudenosaunee and the other represents the Europeans. The Haudenosaunee are traveling in their canoe with the laws and traditions of the Haudenosaunee people. The Europeans are traveling with the laws and traditions which govern them. The path of each is separate but equal.

The Haudenosaunee and the Europeans had a very different understanding of nature. Native people respected the earth and did not think of it as something that could be owned. In the European culture, land was considered property. This different way of thinking about nature led to great confusion and hardship. Hundreds of years later, conflicts arising from this misunderstanding continue to be debated in courtrooms and classrooms across New York State.

John Peter Zenger
Freedom of the Press

John Peter Zenger was only a boy when he emigrated from Germany to New York. He later became a printer's apprentice and in 1733 was appointed publisher of the *New York Weekly Journal*.

Many of the articles that appeared in the *Weekly Journal* criticized New York's governor, William Cosby. They said Governor Cosby was ill-tempered and haughty and did not govern fairly. Under English law it was illegal to make statements that stirred public outrage.

John Zenger did not write the articles and poems which appeared in his newspaper, but as publisher he was responsible for its contents. Zenger was imprisoned for printing articles criticizing Governor Cosby.

A Philadelphia attorney, Andrew Hamilton, defended Zenger. Hamilton compared power to a great river. Kept within its boundaries, it was beautiful. But when the river overflowed its banks, it brought destruction. Hamilton insisted that those who valued freedom must speak out against those who abused power. They must speak the truth or perish.

Hamilton was an eloquent speaker. *It is not the cause of one poor printer, nor of New York alone, which you are now trying,* he argued. *No...every man who prefers freedom to a life of slavery will bless and honor you as men who have baffled the attempt of tyranny.**

The jury agreed with Hamilton. John Zenger was released from prison. This was not just a victory for Zenger or the state of New York. The victory of John Peter Zenger provided the cornerstone for our freedom of the press. It was a victory for the cause of freedom and the voice of truth.

*http://www.law.umkc.edu/faculty/projects/ftrials/zenger/zenger.html

Abraham Lincoln's Beard

One of our most beloved presidents is our 16th president, Abraham Lincoln. His high hat and bearded face are easily recognized by many young Americans.

But Abe Lincoln did not always have a beard. It was an 11-year-old girl, Grace Bedell, from Westfield, New York, who first suggested that Mr. Lincoln might look better if he did.

Hon A B Lincoln...

Dear Sir
My father has just home from the fair and
brought home your picture and Mr. Hamlin's. I
am a little girl only 11 years old, but want you
should be President of the United States very much
so I hope you wont think me very bold to write to
such a great man as you are. Have you any little
girls about as large as I am if so give them my
love and tell her to write to me if you cannot
answer this letter. I have got 4 brother's and part
of them will vote for you any way and if you let
your whiskers grow I will try and get the rest of
them to vote for you would look a great deal better
for your face is so thin. All the ladies like whiskers
and they would tease their husband's to vote for you
and then you would be President. My father is
going to vote for you and if I was a man I would
vote for you to but I will try to get every one to vote

for you that I can I think that rail fence around your picture makes it look very pretty I have got a little baby sister she is nine weeks old and is just as cunning as can be. When you direct your letter direct to Grace Bedell Westfield Chatauque County New York

I must not write any more answer this letter right off

Good bye
Grace Bedell

Private
Miss Grace Bedell

My dear little Miss
Your very agreeable letter of the 15th is
received – I regret the necessity of saying I
have no daughters – I have three sons – one
seventeen, one nine, and one seven years of
age – They, with their mother, constitute
my whole family – As to the whiskers,
having never worn any, do you not think
people would call it a piece of silly affection
if I were to begin it now?

Your very sincere well wisher
A. Lincoln

Although Mr. Lincoln's response to Grace expressed concern that it might seem vain for him to grow a beard, we all know that he did take Grace's advice. After winning the election, Lincoln passed through New York on his way to Washington. President Lincoln asked Grace to come up to the train platform. He stooped down to kiss her, pointed to his beard, and said, "You see, I let these whiskers grow for you, Grace."

Grace Bedell's letter to Lincoln is not the only famous letter from a young New Yorker. In 1897 another little girl, eight-year-old Virginia O'Hanlon from New York City, wrote a letter to the *New York Sun* newspaper asking if there really was a Santa Claus. In one of the most quoted letters of all time, editor Francis P. Church responded, "Yes, Virginia, there is a Santa Claus."

24

New York Is a Mosaic
Annie's Gift

"Ladies first, ladies first!" the burly long-shoreman called to Annie Moore, a rosy-cheeked 17-year-old who had been pushed to the head of the line. It was January 1, 1892, and the new immigration buildings on Ellis Island had just opened.

Annie's younger brothers, Philip and Anthony, followed close behind, not wanting to get lost in the crowd that surrounded them. The trio had come a long way together.

Twelve days before, Annie and her brothers had left their home in Cork County,

Ireland. They were finally going to join their parents, who were waiting for them in America.

Having little money, Annie, Philip, and Anthony made their voyage in steerage, where the poorest passengers traveled. It had been a crowded, foul-smelling journey and many of their fellow travelers had been seasick. "It won't be long," Annie had promised.

Finally she and her brothers had been transferred from the *S.S. Nevada* to the barge which would ferry them to Ellis Island. The lady with the crown and torch waited to welcome them.

A foghorn sounded. Whistles shrieked. Colorful red, white, and blue fabric lined

the wharf. Philip and Anthony didn't know where to look first. "I can't believe we're really here," Annie said. "We finally made it!"

When the plank was set down, the three travelers were escorted to the registration desk. Annie was officially registered and received a $10.00 gold coin to honor her status as the first official immigrant to pass through Ellis Island. She had never before seen a United States coin. She had never before had that much money to call her own!

"I guess that's the best gift you'll ever get," said Philip. Annie smiled. "This coin is a wonderful gift," she said. "But the best gift will be having our family together again. Well, that and being back on dry land!"

Annie Moore, the first immigrant processed at Ellis Island, went on to live a quiet life in the Lower East Side of New York City. She married the son of a German immigrant and had 10 children. She died in 1924 and was buried in an unmarked grave at Calvary Cemetery in Queens, New York.

For decades there was much confusion and misinformation about the real Annie Moore. When genealogical dedication and detective work finally revealed the real Annie Moore, her descendants, as well as supporters from around the country, banded together to find ways to honor our first official immigrant. A chief priority was to provide Annie with a headstone that would be a proper memorial to her young courage.

Mosaic

Sparkling bits of yellow
and pale sky blue
placed and pressed in softened clay,
molded into something new!

Flecks of fiery orange,
bright reddish hues,
placed and pressed in softened clay,
fashioned into something new!

Purple, gray, hunter green,
and all the colors in between,
joyfully placed, gently pressed,
my mosaic family crest!

Even before Annie Moore and her brothers arrived at Ellis Island, people from all over the world settled in New York State. New Yorkers speak many different languages and practice many different religions.

Because many individuals with many different backgrounds and beliefs live inside its borders, in the past New York State was called a cultural melting pot. Others believe that a tossed salad or a patchwork quilt better described our differences. Some believe that a sparkling mosaic might best symbolize our vibrant and diverse culture. What do you think?

New York Months

January brings a bitter chill
to frozen fields and cobbled streets;

but **February** sledding
is a fun-filled winter treat.

March brings a hint of spring
though blustery winds still blow;

April wakes the wild daffodils
that slept beneath the snow.

In **May** the lilacs scent the air
and honeybees are swarming;

by **June** the earth is wide-awake
and city streets are warming.

July brings us ice-cream bells
and beaches hot and sandy;

August days are lazy days
for summer rides and cotton candy.

Then **September** comes and
calls us back to school;

by **October** leaves are falling
and the air is crisp and cool.

November skies are steely blue
and darkness comes too soon;

the old year closes quietly
beneath **December**'s snow-white moon.

Jacob Lawrence & the Harlem Renaissance

During the 1920s and 1930s many African-American families left their rural homes in the South to make new homes in northern cities. Some left to escape floods and the harsh southern heat. For many, sharecropping and tenant farming had become more difficult; some workers left the South to look for jobs in northern factories.

Others left to escape cruel Jim Crow laws that forced whites and blacks to go to separate schools, eat in separate restaurants, and even drink from separate water fountains. Discrimination against blacks often led to violence. Some blacks ventured north hoping to be treated more fairly. Many ended up in a small section of New York City known as Harlem.

The streets of Harlem were not always what those who had migrated north expected. The migrants were not always treated kindly. The streets were noisy and crowded, teeming with activity. But for some, a cement sidewalk could be as fertile as a freshly tilled garden. That's how it was for young Jacob Lawrence.

Jacob Lawrence arrived in Harlem when he was 13. The bright colors and dazzling new shapes of the city inspired him. The sound of a train rumbling overhead awakened the artist in Lawrence. Jacob Lawrence became one of the most famous artists of the Harlem Renaissance, a period of great African-American achievement in art, literature, and music.

Like the sound of the train rumbling over-head, the migration north was the rising heartbeat of a generation of artists, writers, and musicians. For Lawrence, the train became a unifying theme in one of his most famous series of paintings, the Migration Series.

The Migration paintings trace the exodus of African-Americans as they leave the South, but Lawrence captures the universal struggle of all people who search for free-dom, acceptance, and a sense of community. Some Migration panels are part of the permanent collection at the Museum of Modern Art in New York City.

Harlem Tune

Movin' north
through flood and heat,
movin' north
to find my beat,

Rumble, razzle
scat 'n slide,

now Harlem is my home.

Colors bold 'n
colors bright.
Trumpets callin'
out all night.
I'm so glad to be alive—
now Harlem is my home.

Rumble, razzle
scat 'n slide,

I'm so glad to be alive—
'cause Harlem is my home!

A Boy Named Teedie

Theodore (Teddy) Roosevelt, the 26th president of the United States, was born in New York City on October 27, 1858. Roosevelt was a naturalist and a true conservationist. He loved nature and knew how important it was to preserve our country's natural resources. Many of our state lands which have been designated "forever wild" are the result of Teddy's efforts.

Teddy Roosevelt was a rugged outdoorsman. He hiked, he hunted, and, as president, he sometimes swam in the icy waters of the Potomac River. But our 26th president wasn't always so strong and muscular. As a child, Teedie (as his family called him) was often sick. He had poor eyesight and suffered from frequent headaches and severe asthma. Bullies teased him.

Teedie's father told him that he had a good mind, but that he would need to work hard to develop a stronger body. It was hard work but Teedie exercised daily. He even took boxing lessons. He still suffered from asthma but his body became stronger.

When Teedie was still a child, he created the Roosevelt Museum of Natural History. He collected feathers, rocks, insects, even a snakeskin and the skull of a seal. Whenever Teedie went outside, he was on the lookout for new items to display in his museum. He kept a journal of scientific notes to explain his findings.

Teddy Roosevelt's interest in the natural world did not stop when he grew older. While president, Roosevelt worked hard to protect and conserve our natural resources by establishing numerous wildlife reserves and national parks.

A Girl Named Sybil

Sybil Ludington was a 16-year-old Revolutionary War hero, sometimes referred to as the female Paul Revere. Two years after Paul Revere took his famous ride, Sybil Ludington also climbed a horse to muster troops against the British.

Until the night of April 26, 1777, Sybil was an ordinary girl growing up in Putnam County, New York. As the oldest in a big colonial family, Sybil had many chores. She made soap and candles, churned butter, baked bread, and helped her mother take care of her younger siblings.

One rainy April night there was a knock at the door. Nearby Danbury, Connecticut, was in flames. Much of the food and medicine for the rebel troops was stored there. The messenger begged Sybil's father, Colonel Ludington, to gather his men and help defend Danbury.

Colonel Ludington's troops were scattered in houses and farms for miles around. He knew he could not gather his troops and organize them at the same time. He also knew that the messenger at his door was cold and tired and might not find his way on such a dark, rainy night. Who could he send to muster the troops?

Sybil Ludington bravely climbed on her horse, Star. She rode all night, through the dark and the rain, on narrow, bumpy roads. By morning about 400 men had gathered at Ludington's house. Although it was too late to save Danbury, Ludington's troops did stop the British advance in the Battle of Ridgefield.

Ode to New York

Beneath the distant twinkling stars
crickets strum on small guitars;
but in the city ever light,
car horns toot throughout the night.

Above tall buildings that scrape the sky,
gray-gowned pigeons sweep and fly;
while above the trees that brush the clouds,
tuxedoed crows dive and bow.

Apples from the orchard store
are *crunch-i-licious* from skin to core;
but the city's best brown-bag treat
are roasted chestnuts sold on the street.

The scent of crushed magnolia bark
sweetens the path in Central Park;
while on the farm we follow the way
of fresh-tilled earth and new-mown hay.

Open country roads are bumpy,
narrow cobbled streets are lumpy;
but in city place or country space
the sun shines warm upon my face!

Forever Wild Amendment

Before 1894 the unlimited logging of trees had begun to destroy the landscape of the Adirondack and Catskill forests. New York's great wilderness was in ruins. Mud and sludge had seeped into the Mohawk and Hudson rivers, choking transportation of our major waterways.

Many people believed that it was our responsibility to take care of nature. But the tanning industry needed the hemlock. The paper industry needed the spruce. Many loggers and farmers did not want the state involved in land preservation. People argued. Land was logged and left to waste. Fires often started from the sparks of passing trains. The beaver and

the bear were losing their natural habitats. Our sparkling waters were no longer fresh and overflowing.

A lawyer named Verplanck Colvin spent most of his free time exploring the Adirondacks. He made maps and guides. It was Colvin who first discovered Lake Tear in the Clouds, the small tarn at the top of Mount Marcy where the Hudson River begins her journey through New York.

Colvin and other naturalists convinced people of the need to protect New York's natural resources. Finally, in 1894, the "forever wild" amendment was added to our state constitution.

> *The lands of the state, now owned or hereafter*
> *acquired, constituting the forest preserve as now*
> *fixed by law, shall be forever kept as wild forest*
> *lands. They shall not be leased, sold or exchanged,*
> *or be taken by any corporation, public or private,*
> *nor shall the timber thereon be sold, removed,*
> *or destroyed.*

In the beginning the law made little difference. Loggers and hunters continued to spoil the land. But eventually our trees grew lush enough for the beaver and the bear to thrive. The waters washed themselves clean again.

The state lands known as the forest preserve are protected, but there are other natural resources that also need our protection. Ever-evolving environmental laws remind us to keep our forests natural and our waterways fresh and clean.

Soft White Feathers

Soft white feathers
falling down,
over fields
and
over towns.

On country roads
and city streets,
soft white feathers
beneath
my feet.

A Snowy Surprise

A Promise of Spring

Spring is coming soon," Anna said to her father. "I can feel it." Anna and her father had spent a wonderful day together. The circus was in town and they had walked all the way to Madison Avenue to see the parade of elephants march through the city streets.

Anna liked walking with her father. Sometimes he walked so fast that Anna's side ached but he always slowed down if Anna asked him. Besides, his hands were so warm and strong that Anna didn't mind being tugged along.

Today leaves were beginning to blossom on the trees in the park, and flowers were beginning to poke through the earth. Soon she and her family would take lots of walks together.

As Anna and her father got closer to their apartment the air grew misty and dark. It began to rain lightly. "I'm glad Mama stayed home," Anna said. "Otherwise, her cough might have gotten worse!"

A Strange Whiteness

The next morning Anna woke up very early. Everything was quiet. She snuggled under her covers but a soft swooshing sound kept her from falling back to sleep. Even before she opened her eyes, Anna sensed a bright whiteness that filled every corner of her room. She pushed off her blanket and ran to the window.

There was snow everywhere. Telegraph and telephone wires sagged in heavy, tangled white webs. How could so much snow fall so quickly? Just yesterday flowers were poking through the earth and spring seemed days away.

Anna ran to wake her mother and father but they were already awake. Mama was in her robe and slippers but Papa was already dressed and had his doctor's bag ready.

"Mrs. Martorano will be having her baby today," he said. "I need to get across town before the snow is too high."

Anna looked out the window. The snow was already too high. Across the street it drifted higher than the doorways, and the lower apartment windows were

completely blocked. Anna was glad that
she lived in an upstairs apartment where
she could still look out on the street
below. The avenue was empty but snow
continued to fall and swirl. She wished
her father would stay safely at home.

Bundling Up

Anna watched as her father pulled an extra pair of heavy wool socks over his feet. He buttoned every button of his thick woolen vest and stuffed the bottom of his pants into his boots. Her mother helped him put on his heavy gray coat. She pulled up his fur-lined collar and pulled his fur hat down below his ears. Then she tied a scarf around his neck. All Anna could see were her father's twinkling eyes.

"Well, I should certainly be warm enough but I do hope I can move," Papa said, laughing. Her mother laughed, too, but Anna could tell that she was worried.

"Be careful. Turn back if the wind is too harsh. We need you, too."

"I know. I will be careful." Papa looked at Anna. "Anna, you take good care of Mama while I'm gone." Then, taking the coal shovel, he left.

Anna and her mother waited a long time at the window before they saw Papa make his way to the street. His head was bent into his collar. Without looking up Papa turned to wave at them. Together they watched as he pushed his way into the storm. After a long while he was only a small black speck in the snowy distance.

A Mysterious Brown Bundle

For the rest of the morning Anna played with her rag doll while her mother made bread pudding. "Let's look outside," Anna said to her doll. A brown package was being tossed by the wind. Anna watched it lift, swirl, and land in the snow right outside her apartment. She was wondering what sort of package it could be when it moved again.

"Mama, Mama!" she cried. "Hurry, Mama!"

Anna and her mother quickly bundled themselves in a double layer of clothing and ventured into the white wilderness.

The path that Papa had shoveled was already covered but Anna and Mama had brought two skillets from the kitchen to use as shovels. The wind blew in Anna's face like a thousand tiny needles. Her back ached from stooping so low to shovel. Finally they carved a narrow path to the small, brown, crumpled heap that Anna had seen blowing in the wind.

"We're here to help you," Anna said as her mother gently lifted a child into her arms.

A Warm Fire and a Snow-Covered Stranger

Mama settled the child by the fire while Anna brought in a thick wool afghan from her bed. She and her mother wrapped the afghan around the small girl.

"You warm yourself by the fire," Anna's mother said, "while I get you some hot tea."

"Thank you. My name is Sarah."

Sarah looked so small and young. Still, Anna thought, shouldn't she have known better than to go out in a snowstorm wearing only a hooded woolen cape?

"Papa left early this morning to try and get us more coal," Sarah explained. "We were so cold! And we were hungry, too."

"When he didn't come back, I went to look for him. It was so cold and the snow was blowing so hard that I couldn't see. I tried to go back home but the snow made every-thing look different. And the wind! Two times it picked me up and blew me away."

"I saw you—it looked like you were fly-ing!" Anna said.

Sarah continued. "I don't know where I've landed! I'm so lost! My father will never find me." She looked like she was about to cry.

But just then Mama walked in with a tray holding two cups of tea and two big but-ter cookies. She placed the tray on a small wooden table beside the couch and sat down next to Sarah.

"You've landed in a very safe place," she said kindly. "And as soon as Anna's father gets home, we will look for your father."

Waiting for Papa

For the next few hours Anna and Sarah sat by the fire talking. Anna began to understand why Sarah hadn't dressed more warmly. These must be Sarah's warmest clothes.

Anna thought of her heavy woolen coat with the fur collar and the beautiful white muff that her grandmother had given her for Christmas. It made her sad to think that not everyone had warm clothes and enough to eat. But Sarah didn't seem to mind.

"We don't have a fireplace," she said. "But we have a coal stove and when we have enough coal, it's warm and cozy. Papa tells me stories about my mother. She died

when I was born but Papa said I look just like her."

"My father likes to tell me stories, too," Anna said.

When Sarah and Anna had finished their tea they went to the window. Snow was still falling heavily and the wind continued to howl. Now the drifts crawled halfway up the buildings. Anna shivered.

"I wonder where Papa is," Anna and Sarah said in unison.

Two Snow-Covered Creatures

It was still snowing late in the afternoon. Anna could tell that her mother was getting worried.

"Your father should be home soon," Mama said, breathing deeply. Anna could only see thick white flakes swirling furiously against the darkening sky.

"Your father should be home soon," her mother said again as she closed the curtains. "Why don't you show Sarah your new tea set?"

Anna and Sarah were arranging the small china cups on the floor when they heard a loud stomping of feet. They rushed to the front door just as Mama was opening it.

"Papa!" Anna and Sarah shouted at once. There at the door stood two snow-covered creatures. One wore a heavy wool coat trimmed in fur. The other wore a shabby brown jacket with a frayed hem. Both were covered with ice and snow. Mama ushered them inside and closed the door.

"How did you know I was here?" Sarah asked.

"I didn't," her father answered. Like Sarah, her father was small and skinny. His eyebrows were crusted with ice.

"I was looking for you when this kind gentleman persuaded me to come home with him. He was going to give me something warmer to wear while I searched for you."

Sarah's father looked at Anna. "It seems your father has given me something more precious than a coat." He stooped down to kiss Sarah. "But how did you get here?"

"I flew here," Sarah laughed.

"We can talk about it by the fire," Mama said. "You and Sarah will stay with us until the storm is over."

Anna and Sarah looked at each other and smiled. Sarah would stay until the storm was over but she and Anna would be friends for much longer.

September 11, 2001

September 11, 2001 started out as a beautiful fall day. It was sunny, bright, and full of promise. By midmorning everything changed. Darkness filled the sky and smoke billowed through the streets of lower Manhattan. Two hijacked planes had purposely crashed into the landmark skyscrapers known as the Twin Towers. Despite the heroic efforts of firefighters, police, paramedics, and other brave New Yorkers, thousands of people died.

Where are the stars on this dark, dark night?
Where is their tiny twinkling light?
Where is the music?
Where is the song?
Where are the colors?
Something is wrong.

Sometimes stars hide in the clouds,
and their light seems far away.
Sometimes voices are hushed and still,
and the rainbow fades to gray.

Sometimes the world is topsy-turvy,
and nobody really knows why;
Sometimes sad things happen,
and even grown-ups cry.

But always, my child, always,
you are safe here in my arms.
The world may be topsy-turvy,
but I will shelter you from harm.

Always the stars are twinkling,
even when clouds hide their light;
I promise you voices will sing again,
and colors will again shine bright.

I promise there is always tomorrow
for starlight and rainbows and song;
My love will always surround you,
unchanged, unbroken, and strong.

A New York Timeline

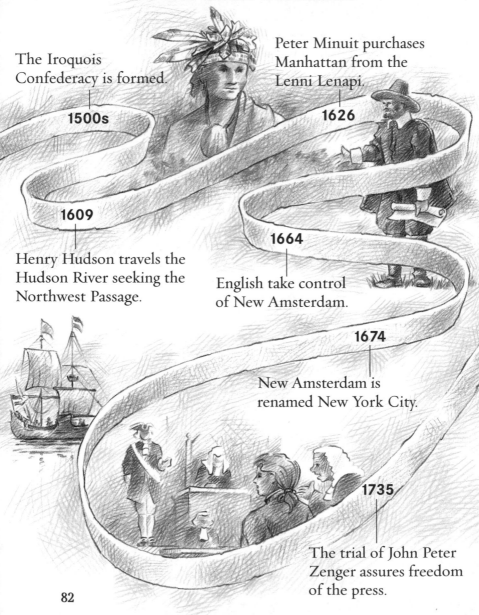

The Iroquois Confederacy is formed.

1500s

Peter Minuit purchases Manhattan from the Lenni Lenapi.

1626

1609

Henry Hudson travels the Hudson River seeking the Northwest Passage.

1664

English take control of New Amsterdam.

1674

New Amsterdam is renamed New York City.

1735

The trial of John Peter Zenger assures freedom of the press.

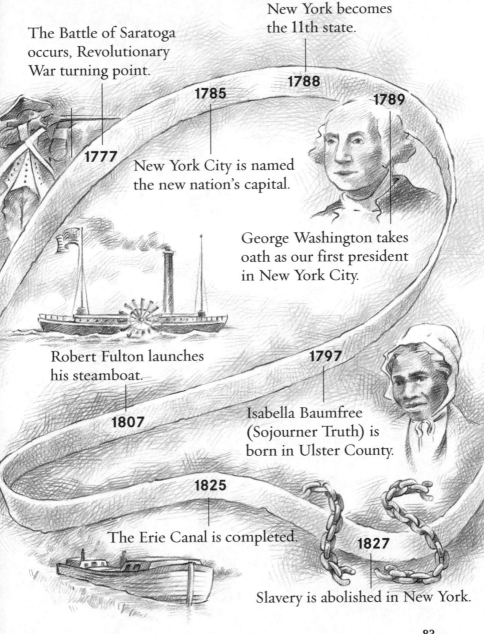

The Battle of Saratoga occurs, Revolutionary War turning point.

1777

1785

New York City is named the new nation's capital.

New York becomes the 11th state.

1788

1789

George Washington takes oath as our first president in New York City.

Robert Fulton launches his steamboat.

1807

1797

Isabella Baumfree (Sojourner Truth) is born in Ulster County.

1825

The Erie Canal is completed.

1827

Slavery is abolished in New York.

83

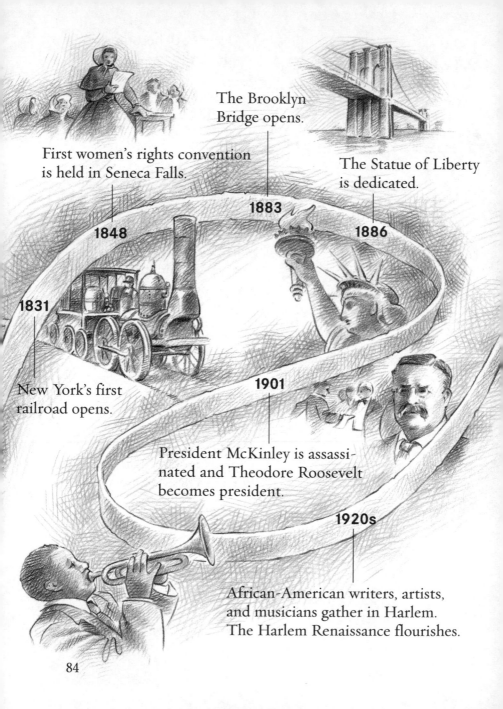

The Brooklyn Bridge opens.

First women's rights convention is held in Seneca Falls.

The Statue of Liberty is dedicated.

1883

1848

1886

1831

New York's first railroad opens.

1901

President McKinley is assassinated and Theodore Roosevelt becomes president.

1920s

African-American writers, artists, and musicians gather in Harlem. The Harlem Renaissance flourishes.

The New York Stock Exchange crashes; the Great Depression begins.

1929

1947

Jackie Robinson plays first base for the Brooklyn Dodgers.

1952

The United Nations Headquarters completed.

1993

Terrorists attack the World Trade Center.

NY's first African-American governor takes office.

2001

2003

2008

A second terrorist attack occurs at the World Trade Center.

Major power outage across eastern United States and Canada.

I Am a Citizen of New York

I am a citizen of New York. What I think and what I say is important. How I treat others is important, too.

I will be tolerant. Everyone has the right to follow his or her own path.

I will be considerate. I will treat people with kindness and be gentle with the earth and all of its creatures.

I will be honest. I will tell the truth even when it is hard. If I make a promise, I will keep it.

I will be fair. Not everyone has the same talents; I will not treat some people as if they were more important than others.

I will be responsible. I will always try my best, but if I make a mistake, I will admit it. I will not blame others.

I will be brave. Doing the right thing is
not always easy, but I will help and defend
those in need.

I am a proud citizen of New York. I am a
student of history, but I am also a part of
history. I will try my best to make the
world a better place.

Ann E. Burg

Ann Burg has been writing since early childhood but did not pursue a writing career full time until 2003. She has been happily writing ever since! *The New York Reader* is Ann's eighth book and her fourth title with Sleeping Bear Press. Ann and her husband live in upstate New York with their two children, a tattered bear, and an ill-behaved but well-loved dog named Smudges.

K. L. Darnell

K. L. (Kate) Darnell cannot remember a time when she did not draw pictures and she counts herself lucky indeed to be doing what she loves for a living. Kate earned a BFA degree studying drawing and painting at the University of Michigan School of Art & Design and has been a professional illustrator for over 25 years, drawing everything from the bottom of a foot to fiddle parts and dinosaurs. *The New York Reader* is her ninth children's book for Sleeping Bear Press. In addition to her illustration work, Kate also specializes in the art of calligraphy, and is a part-time faculty member at Lansing Community College, where she teaches both illustration and calligraphy. She lives and works—just a bicycle ride away—in East Lansing, Michigan.